Figures of Speech

FIGURES OF SPEECH

meryl phair

ISBN 978-0-578-30845-6

Edited and designed by Tell Tell Poetry

Printed in the United States of America

First Printing, 2022

Contents

it is impossible for me to describe concrete poetry in a few sentences, but i feel it is relevant because it is concerned with intelligence & order, not the self, 'thought' and fuss ... the aim should be choice - i.e. the measure of science & the arts should be decency, not ... self-dramatization.

ian hamilton finlay

Figures of Speech

table of contents

word:
noun

1. meaningful element of speech or writing, used with others (or sometimes alone) to form a sentence

2. unit of language, comprising inflected and variant forms

3. something that someone says or writes; a remark or piece of information

4. speech as distinct from action

5. the smallest amount of something spoken or written

6. person's account of the truth, especially when it differs from that of another person (one's word)

7. a promise or assurance

8. the text or spoken part of a play, opera, or other performed piece, a script

9. angry talk

10. a message, news

word:
verb

11. choose and use particular words in order to say or write (something), to word

word
noun

1. meaningful element of speech or writing,
used with others (or sometimes alone) to form a sentence

relation
ships

little
paper boats
beating down
the
currents ink printed skin
slowly dissolving

little
paper boats
beating down
the
currents ink printed skin
slowly dissolving

knowledge

you could still fall off any k n o w n l
e
d
g
e

habit

v e
o r
c s
your body
in folds

t h

r

to

desire o

overwhelming

an w

have

i o

height

great f

a

at f

standing

i'm i

whenever

t

m

o e

t

s

h

n

i

g

fragile

flow

i
move
too
fast
a
river
over
rocks
but
if
i
hold
back
i
can't
hold
on
and
if
i
stand
still
i
may
never
move again

the
world
cut off
at its
feet
leaving
you with
no
way to
stand up
on your
own

off cut
its at
feet
leaving
with you
no
to way
up stand
your on
own

the
world
off cut
its at
feet
leaving
with you
no
to way
up stand
your on
own

the
world
cut off
at its
feet
leaving
you with
no
way to
stand up
on your
own

the
world
off cut
its at
feet
leaving
with you
no
to way
up stand
your on
own

the
world
cut off
at its
feet
leaving
you with
no

the
world
cut off
at its
feet
leaving
you with
no
way to
stand up
on your
own

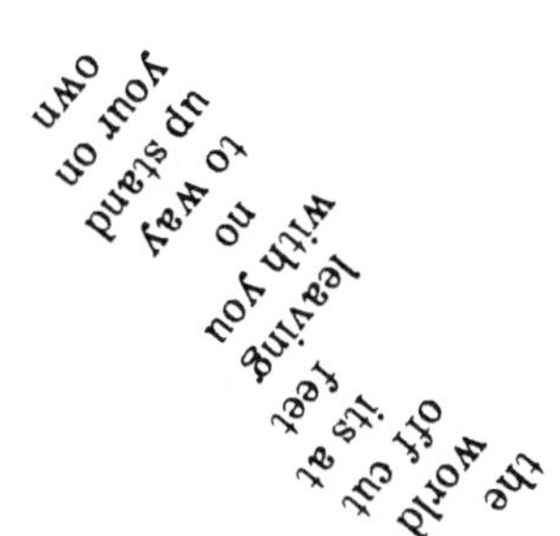

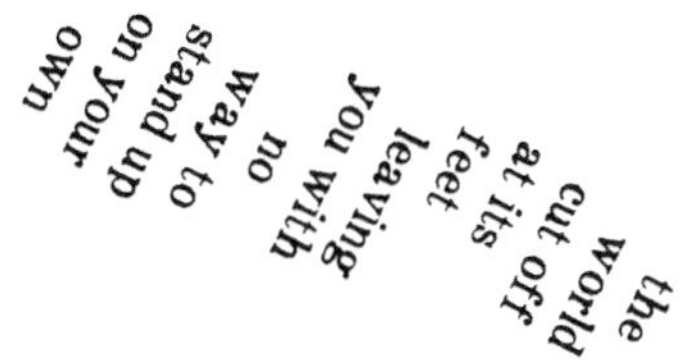

the
world
off cut
its at
feet
leaving
with you
no
to way
up stand
your on
own

the
world
cut off
at its
feet
leaving
you with
no
way to
stand up
on your
own

defeated

c

e

h c

e

h

c

o h

o

e

o

s

e

s

s

e

distance

i
am
so
far
a

way

building
blocks

to

up knock

them them

pile d

o

w

n

cit(e)scapes

i built
cities from
ruins their
luminescence scaffolding up into the stars

2. unit of language,
comprising inflected and variant forms

i d

r g

b e

a d

r i

b d

g

a e

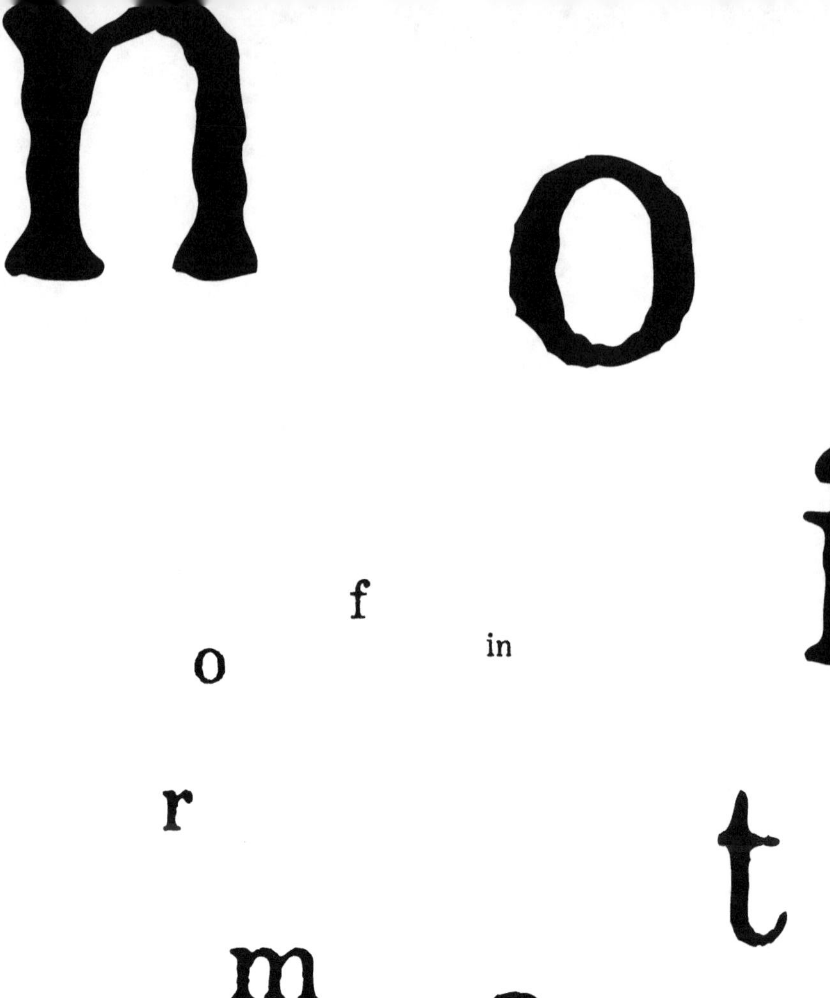
n
o
i
f
in
o
r
t
m
a

v sub ersive

f

a

l

l

a. part

l o n g i

a. long

b. long

n g

p a

i r

a

d i

s e

i lost my

t r a i n o f t h o

u

g

h

t

it went off track

stretching

t h

e

t

r

u

h

t

l

e

t

d

o

w

n

i

t

o

u

n to the wind

a

throw c

3. something that someone says or writes
a remark or piece of information

conversation found
crepes and coffee

i
will
sit
in
artisan
roast
refresh
the
mind
the
flow
b
a
l
l
o
o
n
s
for
me
for
you
how will i know when it gets here
ahh right clearly everything parachutes
it will get to where it is going
do you want a bigger table over there
no i'm fine here with
this one

cloud services

welcome

to your own
non renewable
business
a place to connect
think big
frozen
flower shop
take your seat
rent free
transport yourself to a better place
it's here
it's always
open till late
your life

a space

no more
streets ahead
a take away
zone
repair
individuals
home of irresistible
safety
except
with
no
noise
no through route
stop and look back
look twice
together

we call the world

for less

pleasance

monday through friday
secured on the pink
stucco walls

creative minds

tired of
speed limits
the only thing you do
every time there's
nowhere you'd rather be
sometimes you are
wanted
a left lane
exit
built
to quit
night
roofing
leading the way you could
burn
emergency
bright
lose it
and keep
healing
the words i said to you never got in
community built
nice town
another day
another chance
to switch and

save

world
disorder

we can't
be anything by our selves
no common rules
and regulations
helpless
against
hostile acts
emerging alternative structures
forecast
strategy
withdrawals
big perspectives
systematic competitions
frightening shapes and forms
questions of value
you must do
certain things alone
lose traction
to describe what we are
seeing

when the moment
comes
read history
destroy every thing
on a different
page

thirsty mind

you were little
we were on a beach
you took a handful
of pebbles
shoveled them into your
mouth
said they tasted
like
blueberries
you were always
spooning honey
down your throat
asking questions
without waiting
for the
answers

flutter kicks

do you know anyone here?

no, i've never seen them

have you ever been here before?

no, i don't think so

lake thoughts

1.

when the sun
hits the water
it makes a rainbow
that only you can see

2.

to swim
back and back
around and around
you didn't have to
go far

3.

slimy
weedy
a creature
from the blue lagoon

4.

you can't always
be in the
water

5.

that is how it goes
i am a used to be
you're a never was

bank notes

small business owners
how will you increase
the flexibility of your cash
flow this winter?

how it came through

as a master sculptor
in the
quest for food
the mouth dominates everywhere
to make a statement like
that toe fox
in the cayman islands

and wildlife woods anywhere
is a portal

where the world begins to change
from nonself to self
it's what we
talked
about earlier
about
perception
and the child learning
the road
learning the difference between
the mother

itself
and the rest
of the world

4. speech as distinct from action

a play
words

they set the stage
for you to act upon

when the truth
comes out

the skeletons in the closet
got bored
of hanging themselves

pitfall

the sun

silting through
loosely

held leaves

plum flesh
melting

underneath

losing
purchase

your feet

no longer
owned
the ground
in the same way

as
when
you
bought

it

felt

distinctive
shape comes
from being
stuck through

with pins and

needles

deep-seated claims

they sat low
in the folding chairs
out back

faculty of the mind

they meet and
organize
along neurons
and synapses

employed to advise
you on all types

of m o t i o n

eavesdrop

gabled roof corners
drooped d

o

w

n
to the ground
for
wild bees
to make nests
with

secrets

broadcast

arms aching
from pulling
soaking fish nets
out of the water
trapped wriggling
bodies
scattering
on the deck
watching
as they got
quieter

raising questions

you brought
up these
points
and
now
they're
living

without
you

bear in mind

your thoughts
    have claws

5. the smallest amount of something
spoken or written

i'm pulses

i'm patient

i’m   pressionable

i'm   pressive

im

ages

ngnothingnothingnothingnothingnothingnothingnothingnothingnothingnothingnoth
gnothingnothingnothingnothingnothingnothingnothingnothingnothingnothingnoth
nothingnothingnothingnothingnothingnothingnothingnothingnothingnothingnothir
thingnothingnothingnothingnothingnothingnothingnothingnothingnothingnothing
hingnothingnothingnothingnothingnothingnothingnothingnothingnothingnothingn
ingnothingnothingnothingnothingnothingnothingnothingnothingnothingnothingno
ngnothingnothingnothingnothingnothingnothingnothingnothingnothingnothingnoth
gnothingnothingnothingnothingnothingnothingnothingnothingnothingnothingnoth
nothingnothingnothingnothingnothingnothingnothingnothingnothingnothingnothir
thingnothingnothingnothingnothingnothingnothingnothingnothingnothingnothing
hingnothingnothingnothingnothingnothingnothingnothingnothingnothingnothingn
ingnothingnothingnothingnothingnothingnothingnothingnothingnothingnothingno
ngnothingnothingnothingnothingnothingnothingnothingnothingnothingnothingnoth
gnothingnothingnothingnothingnothingnothingnothingnothingnothingnothingnoth
nothingnothingnothingnothingnothingnothingnothingnothingnothingnothingnothir
thingnothingnothingnothingnothingnothingnothingnothingnothingnothingnothing
hingnothingnothingnothingnothingnothingnothingnothingnothingnothingnothingn
ingnothingnothingnothingnothingnothingnothingnothingnothingnothingnothingno
ngnothingnothingnothingnothingnothingnothingnothingnothingnothingnothingnoth
gnothingnothingnothingnothingnothingnothingnothingnothingnothingnothingnoth
nothingnothingnothingnothingnothingnothingnothingnothingnothingnothingnothir
thingnothingnothingnothingnothingnothingnothingnothingnothingnothingnothing
hingnothingnothingnothingnothingnothingnothingnothingnothingnothingnothingn
ingnothingnothingnothingnothingnothingnothingnothingnothingnothingnothingno
ngnothingnothingnothingnothingnothingnothingnothingnothingnothingnothingnoth
gnothingnothingnothingnothingnothingnothingnothingnothingnothingnothingnoth
nothingnothingnothingnothingnothingnothingnothingnothingnothingnothingnothir
thingnothingnothingnothingnothingnothingnothingnothingnothingnothingnothing
hingnothingnothingnothingnothingnothingnothingnothingnothingnothingnothingn
ingnothingnothingnothingnothingnothingnothingnothingnothingnothingnothingno
ngnothingnothingnothingnothingnothingnothingnothingnothingnothingnothingnoth
gnothingnothingnothingnothingnothingnothingnothingnothingnothingnothingnoth
nothingnothingnothingnothingnothingnothingnothingnothingnothingnothingnothir
thingnothingnothingnothingnothingnothingnothingnothingnothingnothingnothing
hingnothingnothingnothingnothingnothingnothingnothingnothingnothingnothingn
ingnothingnothingnothingnothingnothingnothingnothingnothingnothingnothingno
ngnothingnothingnothingnothingnothingnothingnothingnothingnothingnothingnoth
gnothingnothingnothingnothingnothingnothingnothingnothingnothingnothingnoth
nothingnothingnothingnothingnothingnothingnothingnothingnothingnothingnothir
thingnothingnothingnothingnothingnothingnothingnothingnothingnothingnothing
hingnothingnothingnothingnothingnothingnothingnothingnothingnothingnothingn
ingnothingnothingnothingnothingnothingnothingnothingnothingnothingnothingno
ngnothingnothingnothingnothingnothingnothingnothingnothingnothingnothingnoth
gnothingnothingnothingnothingnothingnothingnothingnothingnothingnothingnoth
nothingnothingnothingnothingnothingnothingnothingnothingnothingnothingnothir
thingnothingnothingnothingnothingnothingnothingnothingnothingnothingnothing
hingnothingnothingnothingnothingnothingnothingnothingnothingnothingnothingn
ingnothingnothingnothingnothingnothingnothingnothingnothingnothingnothingno
ngnothingnothingnothingnothingnothingnothingnothingnothingnothingnothingnoth
gnothingnothingnothingnothingnothingnothingnothingnothingnothingnothingnoth
nothingnothingnothingnothingnothingnothingnothingnothingnothingnothingnothir
thingnothingnothingnothingnothingnothingnothingnothingnothingnothingnothing
hingnothingnothingnothingnothingnothingnothingnothingnothingnothingnothingn
ingnothingnothingnothingnothingnothingnothingnothingnothingnothingnothingno
ngnothingnothingnothingnothingnothingnothingnothingnothingnothingnothingnoth
gnothingnothingnothingnothingnothingnothingnothingnothingnothingnothingnoth
nothingnothingnothingnothingnothingnothingnothingnothingnothingnothingnothir
thingnothingnothingnothingnothingnothingnothingnothingnothingnothingnothing
hingnothingnothingnothingnothingnothingnothingnothingnothingnothingnothingn

no

thing

aughterslaughterslaughterslaughterslaughterslaughterslaughterslaught
laughterslaughterslaughterslaughterslaughterslaughterslaughterslaugh
slaughterslaughterslaughterslaughterslaughterslaughterslaughterslaug
erslaughterslaughterslaughterslaughterslaughterslaughterslaughterslau
terslaughterslaughterslaughterslaughterslaughterslaughterslaughtersla
hterslaughterslaughterslaughterslaughterslaughterslaughterslaughtersl
ghterslaughterslaughterslaughterslaughterslaughterslaughterslaughters
ghterslaughterslaughterslaughterslaughterslaughterslaughterslaughter
ughterslaughterslaughterslaughterslaughterslaughterslaughterslaughte
aughterslaughterslaughterslaughterslaughterslaughterslaughterslaught
laughterslaughterslaughterslaughterslaughterslaughterslaughterslaugh
slaughterslaughterslaughterslaughterslaughterslaughterslaughterslaug
erslaughterslaughterslaughterslaughterslaughterslaughterslaughterslau
terslaughterslaughterslaughterslaughterslaughterslaughterslaughtersla
hterslaughterslaughterslaughterslaughterslaughterslaughterslaughtersl
ghterslaughterslaughterslaughterslaughterslaughterslaughterslaughters
ghterslaughterslaughterslaughterslaughterslaughterslaughterslaughter
ughterslaughterslaughterslaughterslaughterslaughterslaughterslaughte
aughterslaughterslaughterslaughterslaughterslaughterslaughterslaught
laughterslaughterslaughterslaughterslaughterslaughterslaughterslaugh
slaughterslaughterslaughterslaughterslaughterslaughterslaughterslaug
erslaughterslaughterslaughterslaughterslaughterslaughterslaughterslau
terslaughterslaughterslaughterslaughterslaughterslaughterslaughtersla
hterslaughterslaughterslaughterslaughterslaughterslaughterslaughtersl
ghterslaughterslaughterslaughterslaughterslaughterslaughterslaughters
ghterslaughterslaughterslaughterslaughterslaughterslaughterslaughter
ughterslaughterslaughterslaughterslaughterslaughterslaughterslaughte
aughterslaughterslaughterslaughterslaughterslaughterslaughterslaught
laughterslaughterslaughterslaughterslaughterslaughterslaughterslaugh
slaughterslaughterslaughterslaughterslaughterslaughterslaughterslaug
erslaughterslaughterslaughterslaughterslaughterslaughterslaughterslau
terslaughterslaughterslaughterslaughterslaughterslaughterslaughtersla
hterslaughterslaughterslaughterslaughterslaughterslaughterslaughtersl
ghterslaughterslaughterslaughterslaughterslaughterslaughterslaughters
ghterslaughterslaughterslaughterslaughterslaughterslaughterslaughter
ughterslaughterslaughterslaughterslaughterslaughterslaughterslaughte
aughterslaughterslaughterslaughterslaughterslaughterslaughterslaught
laughterslaughterslaughterslaughterslaughterslaughterslaughterslaugh
slaughterslaughterslaughterslaughterslaughterslaughterslaughterslaug
erslaughterslaughterslaughterslaughterslaughterslaughterslaughterslau
terslaughterslaughterslaughterslaughterslaughterslaughterslaughtersla
hterslaughterslaughterslaughterslaughterslaughterslaughterslaughtersl
ghterslaughterslaughterslaughterslaughterslaughterslaughterslaughters
ghterslaughterslaughterslaughterslaughterslaughterslaughterslaughter
ughterslaughterslaughterslaughterslaughterslaughterslaughterslaughte
aughterslaughterslaughterslaughterslaughterslaughterslaughterslaught
laughterslaughterslaughterslaughterslaughterslaughterslaughterslaugh
slaughterslaughterslaughterslaughterslaughterslaughterslaughterslaug
erslaughterslaughterslaughterslaughterslaughterslaughterslaughterslau
terslaughterslaughterslaughterslaughterslaughterslaughterslaughtersla
hterslaughterslaughterslaughterslaughterslaughterslaughterslaughtersl
ghterslaughterslaughterslaughterslaughterslaughterslaughterslaughters
ghterslaughterslaughterslaughterslaughterslaughterslaughterslaughter
ughterslaughterslaughterslaughterslaughterslaughterslaughterslaughte
aughterslaughterslaughterslaughterslaughterslaughterslaughterslaught
laughterslaughterslaughterslaughterslaughterslaughterslaughterslaugh
slaughterslaughterslaughterslaughterslaughterslaughterslaughterslaug
erslaughterslaughterslaughterslaughterslaughterslaughterslaughterslau
terslaughterslaughterslaughterslaughterslaughterslaughterslaughtersla

s   laughter

s words

g

ap

a

far

a

e

r

a

a

void

you

me

over

taking

taking

over

under

stand

stand

under

with

stand

stand

with

under　　　way

way

under

b

r

ok

e

n

am i

i am

are you

you are

are **we**

we
are

6. person's account of the truth,
especially when it differs from that of another person (one's word)

ribcage

dark feathers slide

between the smooth

bone cage

searching for

a way out

regardless

regard

l

s

e

s

parenthetical claim

often i feel like a
parenthetical claim
a nonessential
clarification
of a previous statement
i should be thought of
as circumscribed with commas
i should be known as
the run on

baggages

heavier

with

time

a confession

i write my thoughts
like you say your prayers
religiously
without knowing
why

7. a promise or assurance

you had to do it

g o w

n r

to figure out
how to do it

right

if you go

s d r a w k c a b

you can go

f o r w a r d s

again

h

a

n

g

in
there
keep
holding
on

8. the text or spoken part of a play, opera, or other performed piece

a script

loneliness

sunlight

and

heaviness

the damp air,

dripping,

between

storms

loneliness

is a

different place.

with light filtering

overhead

rain stretching

the

present.

rain stretching

divides

the region,

In several ways

big thing

a general nodding of heads.

was a "big thing,"

the next morning

the next morning is a

very different sound,

heard shortly after dawn.

the world

outside the world.

of noise and big ideas.

without roofs,

without walls, none of them really complete.

the whole thing

left.

to get the whole thing

back.

I would

now

never be able to stay

the other side

left standing,

Somewhere over there,

truth

to convey a world,

and

qualities of truth,

language

use

slightly different

language to join

end to end.

Sometimes this worked well

But

other times the

exchanging was

undefined

the way

and

anything

in some ways,

is

right.

picture

upside down and

outside our own

picture of the world.

honey trees

The

small honey

trees

found it difficult

among the debris,

to take root.

to raise its

leaves

voice

a voice

was

more than a sound

existence

but you will find

it never existed

9. angry talk

black & blue

from adjectives
the nouns you threw
have covered me
in cuts

t

g a

n l

i k

y e l l
e   i
l   n
l i n g

10. a message,
news

the situation
room

our house is on fire
if anyone crosses
our borders
we will hit them
like a drum
no other
art
is used the same way
or to the same
extent

found poem no. 1

The Unglamorous Work of Looking

d ow n a t

a Bridge Collaps e

to Bypa s s

D e M a n d s

r e port of Qu i e t

Writing

What Do We Know About How It Works?

A s T ime Causes a Stir i n t H e

s an d

found poem no. 2

A Story: a small Fish With a Big Enemy a Beach of One's Own

found poem no. 3

Drop Out

Queen Leaving to Start Her Own space Station

found poem no. 4

Grim Aftermath of

Cut Out   s   tar s

found poem no. 5

Once Reluc t a n t
We're Here to gether
a Strong m e s sage
t o Become a r ock
I ve Never Seen Anoth e r
Night t
Where Yes r e ally Means N o

found poem no. 6

old i n side

a Bullet Ends a n Eating Tige r

rain position s e n t

s piral of a Pas t

the st ation ought to Ask About ship s

o i l to live r

p R o tect a Way of Life

l ook a s Hope m ight

E n d

t H e Numbers

The r i s e i s Anything but Typical

found poem no. 7

A Compromise Nobody Lik e s

land can Have a History of i solation

Why the nou n s

Stayed Put and Lived to Tell the Tale

f i r e Finds a Way to

B e th e o nly One Roaring

t o s t e p Aside

i n a Bounce Back

l o se sen c

e Ov e r

Train s

found poem no. 8

Octopus art

e xplosio n i n

T ree Places here t ied to the Border

Tragic History : A Boy, a Gun and the U.S. Marines

Lied Even After Agreeing

The Rise o f

Ringleader Rebell i o n s

Neck So Far ou t

a Push o n to Stage

S t ep Dow n Amid s truggles

y o u Might Not Help

found poem no. 9

ra i s i ng r ed

t o Respond to Yellow

a s te A dy, rain

o f Lone St a r s

a

t u rbulent

I Love Y o u

Now s tamp

Sending s t rangers Could M ea n a

river o ver th e r e

Growth Cools, Leaving Scars Unhealed

We Went to Dinner P le a s e d

found poem no. 10

t h e Image o f
S oil Ach i n g
R o o ted Deep i n
the Blink of an Eye as
Drilling Questions
for Oil Take
Bu t Won't Deliver
A Snowstorm f ol d
Water s n ew Worries
Will i Find
Breathing Room

found poem no. 11

Roots of Word s

a s h ield Fro m

Just Don't Ask About It

Behind a Vas t

Snow Fore st a Path From M e

T o Who i a m

a L e a ned on S e n t en ce

n e w Phase of t urbulen T

Information From t H e c learances

Why y o u

st i ll Fac e

l o st Control

found poem no. 12

a Long-Suffering Home

to Mend Open Wounds

Today, We All Grieve s hooting Victims

Who Wer e Victims Shoot in g

H e re e

i Face a Crossroads

Flood Down t H e Law

o v er O th e r

t o r n s p ace

here the Who's Wh o r ac e t o

Build a way Across s ound

word

verb

11. choose and use particular words in order
to say or write (something), to word

configuration

b

e

n

t

o f

u o s

t h

a

p

e

equilateral

d

e a

i l

r l

t t

i s e l g n a e h

square up

<table>
<tr><td>f</td><td>a</td><td>c</td><td>e</td><td>a</td></tr>
<tr><td>s</td><td></td><td></td><td></td><td>l</td></tr>
<tr><td>e</td><td></td><td></td><td></td><td>l</td></tr>
<tr><td>d</td><td></td><td></td><td></td><td>y</td></tr>
<tr><td>i</td><td>s</td><td>r</td><td>u</td><td>o</td></tr>
</table>

sphere

h

m e

a r

i e

rectangle

i w r e c k e d

s a

e l

l g n a e h t l

trapezoid

t r a p p e d

d i

i n

o v a

polygone

e

n n

o o

g g

o o

n n

e

scalene

e

l　l

e　a

a

c

n

i　n　t　o　t　h　e　s

spiral

o
u

t
o

f

c

o

n

t

r

o

l

be there or be square

b

or

b b

b b

in any shape or form

i n

a n y

or

i

n

a n

y

comes in all shapes and sizes

e s

m i

o n

a l l c a

l l

n o

i s e m e s i

o n

c a

l

l

taking shape

t a k i n g

s h

a p

e

m o

f

r

o

r

f

f

m m

m

r o

r r

m

o

o r

r

o

f

r o

f

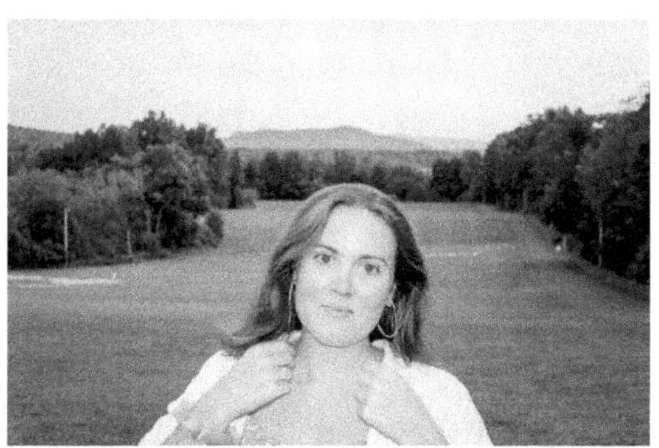

Meryl Phair is currently pursuing her master's degree in magazine & digital storytelling at New York University's Arthur L. Carter Journalism Institute. She previously attended Mount Holyoke College in Massachusetts, graduating with a bachelor's degree in journalism & media. Along with her passion for journalism, Phair's love of writing has led her to explore poetry. She attended an international writing program at the University of Edinburgh in 2018, which inspired her interest in the field of visual and concrete work. She self-published her first two collections of poetry, *Figures of Speech* and *beeing*, with Tell Tell Poetry in 2021. Phair lives in New York, where she reads, runs, and writes.

www.ingramcontent.com/pod-product-compliance
Lightning Source LLC
LaVergne TN
LVHW010608100826
845148LV00014B/2889

* 9 7 8 0 5 7 8 3 0 8 4 5 6 *